04/99   20080300   13.95

BASEBALL

BASEBALL: THE POSITIONS

BRYANT LLOYD

The Rourke Press Inc.
Vero Beach, Florida 32964

PHOTO CREDITS:
All photos © Lynn M. Stone except page 22 © Chris Luneski

EDITORIAL SERVICES:
Penworthy Learning Systems

Library of Congress Cataloging-in-Publication Data

Lloyd, Bryant, 1942-
   Baseball, the positions / Bryant Lloyd.
      p. cm. — (Baseball)
   Includes index
   Summary: Discusses the positions in the game of baseball, including pitcher, catcher, infielders and outfielders.
      ISBN 1-57103-187-1
      1. Fielding (Baseball)—Juvenile literature. [1. Fielding (Baseball). 2. Baseball.]
   I. Title II. Series: Lloyd, Bryant, 1942- Baseball.
   GV870.L56 1997
   796.357'2—dc21   97–17454
                                                                    CIP
                                                                    AC

Printed in the USA

TABLE OF CONTENTS

The Positions 5

The Catcher 6

The Pitcher 8

First Baseman 11

Second Baseman 12

Shortstop 14

Third Baseman 17

Center Fielder 18

Right and Left Fielders 20

Glossary 23

Index 24

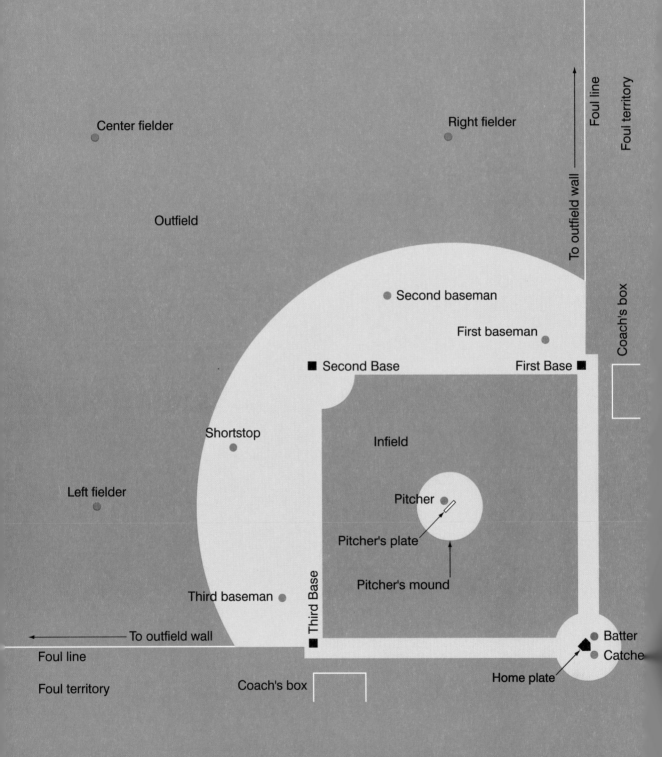

THE POSITIONS

While one baseball team bats, the other team is on the field. That team—the **defensive** (di FEN siv) team—has nine players in different places, or positions.

The defensive team has a pitcher, catcher, and four other **infielders** (IN FEEL derz). It also has three **outfielders** (OUT FEEL derz).

The pitcher and catcher must begin play at certain places on the field. The other fielders can move around. Usually, however, they play in one general area.

Whenever the great left-handed hitter Ted Williams was at bat, opposing teams often moved their third baseman to shortstop and the shortstop behind second base. The maneuver became known as the "Williams Shift."

This diagram shows the team positions on a baseball field.

THE CATCHER

The catcher crouches behind home plate in an area five feet (1 1/2 meters) long called the **catcher's box** (KACH erz BAHKS). The catcher's main job is to catch pitches that the batter does not hit.

A catcher has to follow the flight of the pitched ball carefully. If the batter doesn't hit the pitch, the catcher needs to catch it.

A third baseman guards the runner at third and gives his catcher a glove target. Quick throws from catchers can catch runners off base.

The catcher helps the pitcher decide what kind of pitch to throw and where to throw it. The catcher's glove becomes the pitcher's target.

The catcher sometimes must throw to a base. Catchers also must be ready to scoop up balls hit near them.

THE PITCHER

The pitcher throws, or pitches, the baseball toward a batter. If the batter does not hit the pitch, the catcher usually catches it.

The pitcher throws from a low mound on the center of the infield. One foot must stay on the **pitching rubber** (PICH ing RUB er) on the mound.

The pitcher must be ready to field any ball hit to that position. If the first baseman cannot cover first base, the pitcher must do it.

A pitcher follows through on a pitch. His strong forward motion carries his foot off the pitching rubber.

FIRST BASEMAN

The first baseman must catch throws from other infielders. He wears a special, oversized glove for this job.

The first baseman must also field ground balls and fly balls near first base.

The first baseman is often an especially tall player. A tall player's glove will reach a fielder's throw a split second sooner than would a shorter players' glove. Height also allows a first baseman to reach farther for throws to first base.

A pitcher can control the outcome of a game. Managers of major league teams have said that "pitching is 75 percent of the game."

A first baseman (yellow uniform) guards the first base line. He helps keep the runner close to the base by being ready for a quick throw.

SECOND BASEMAN

The second baseman sets up about midway between first and second base to field every ground ball or fly ball within reach. On some plays, this player runs to second base to take a throw.

A second baseman rushes to make a play on a slowly hit ground ball.

Having taken the right fielder's throw, the second baseman throws the ball to the plate. A good throw from the second baseman may catch the runner (yellow uniform) who is streaking toward the plate.

The second baseman must also be a "cutoff man" on long hits. That means the second baseman runs part way into the outfield, takes a throw from an outfielder, and throws the ball to another infielder.

SHORTSTOP

The shortstop plays midway between second and third base. A shortstop needs a strong arm and excellent fielding skills. Handling more hit balls than other fielders, a shortstop has a fairly long throw to first base.

The shortstop covers second base on balls hit to the right side of the infield and sometimes has to be a "cutoff man." The shortstop also must be ready to cover second base. If a runner attempts to **steal** (STEEL), the shortstop also must be ready to cover second base.

Because most people are right-handed and bat right-handed, more ground balls are hit to shortstop than other infield positions.

A shortstop throws the baseball to the first baseman.

THIRD BASEMAN

The third baseman usually plays close to third base. If a batter **bunts** (BUNTS) the ball toward third base, the third baseman must charge toward home plate.

The third base position is called the "hot corner." Many balls hit toward third base are struck very hard. Third base is just 90 feet (27 meters) from the batter!

The third baseman has the longest throw to first base of any infielder. This throw takes sure hands and a powerful arm.

A hard hit ground ball to third base can make anyone blink, even a young third baseman.

CENTER FIELDER

The center fielder, the captain of the outfield, plays in the middle of the outfield, more or less behind second base.

The center fielder usually has the strongest arm and the most speed among the outfielders.

A center fielder chases down a fly ball.

A center fielder rises up to throw to the infielder (far left) after picking up the ball.

A center fielder must be able to cover more outfield territory than the left or right fielders.

A center fielder must pick up ground balls and catch fly balls. If another outfielder drops a ball, the center fielder has to be nearby.

RIGHT AND LEFT FIELDERS

The right and left fielders must have strong, accurate arms. They must be able to throw to second base, third base, home plate, or a "cutoff man." The right fielder usually gets balls hit by left-handed hitters. Right-handed hitters hit more often to the left fielder.

Outfielders need to be good judges of fly balls, especially on windy days. They must also be always alert for bad throws that roll from the infield positions into the outfield.

Baseball began with a game known as rounders. Runners weren't tagged, though. They were out only when they were hit by fielders' throws. The game began to change into a more modern form in 1845 in New York City.

An outfielder's job is to throw the ball back into the infield as soon as he gets it.

GLOSSARY

bunt (BUNT) — to tap a pitched ball just a few feet into fair territory

catcher's box (KACH erz BAHKS) — the white-lined, rectangular area behind home plate in which a catcher takes pitches

defensive (di FEN siv) — the team on the field trying to keep batters from scoring

infielder (IN FEEL derz) — any of the six players in infield positions, especially the first baseman, second baseman, third baseman, and shortstop

outfielder (OUT FEEL derz) — one who plays in the outfield on a baseball team; the right fielder, center fielder, and left fielder

pitching rubber (PICH ing RUB er) — the rectangular block of rubber on the mound, against which a pitcher must put one foot when pitching

steal (STEEL) — the process of taking a base during the pitcher's windup and pitch; taking a base during or between pitches without a hit ball

INDEX

base   7

baseball   8

batter   6, 8, 17

catcher   5, 6, 7, 8

catcher's box   6

center fielder   18, 19

"cutoff man"   13, 14, 20

fielders   14

first base   8, 11, 12, 14, 17

first baseman   8, 11

fly ball   11, 12, 18, 19, 20

glove   7, 11

ground ball   11, 12, 18

hitters (see batter)

home plate   17, 20

infield   8, 14

infielders   5, 11, 13

left fielder   18, 20

mound   8

outfield   13, 20

outfielders   5, 13, 18, 19, 20

pitcher   5, 7, 8

pitching rubber   8

positions   5

right fielder   19, 20

runner   14

second base   12, 14, 18, 20

second baseman   12, 13

shortstop   14

third base   14, 17, 20

third baseman   14, 17

throws   11, 12, 13, 14, 17, 20